Innocence…

Constance Turner

BookLeaf
Publishing

India | USA | UK

Presentation by *BookLeaf Publishing*

Web: www.bookleafpub.com

E-mail: info@bookleafpub.com

ISBN: 978-93-5744-858-1

First edition 2022

DEDICATION

I dedicate this book to all who aim to understand why their innocence was lost.

ACKNOWLEDGEMENT

I'm so grateful to God for knowing that my loss was His gain. I acknowledge that the loss of my innocence caused my pain, yet much gain. Eternal gain is the ultimate goal!

PREFACE

As a child we never imagine that one day you are innocently playing with dolls or action figures; your only desire is to play outside in the neighborhood kickball, football, softball or a basketball game. Suddenly, life changes with one touch, one look, and innocence is gone.

In the beginning

Ponytails and pigtails
Baby dolls and balls
Board games and books
Cupcakes and cookies
Simple, innocent eight year old loves…gone

WHY?

People always asking me why?
I don't know why, why me and not somebody
else.
I always thought big brothers took care...
I'm eight, chunky, with ponytails and I eat
pancakes.
I played kickball, and basketball.
Ask him WHY!

The grey light

It's time to go to sleep my daddy would say from outside my closed bedroom door. I'd quickly lean over and turn down the light on the black and white. You see the volume was already down, but my grey light, that was my security; my protection from the dark. It was just enough for me to read. As long as I was reading, no one was coming and touching or taking my innocence. My grey light, my secret security.

Sixth Sense

Me: "Mommy, I don't like him!
Mommy: "Why? You don't like nobody!"
Me:"I don't know, it's something; but y'all never believe me. I'll be quiet!"
Two weeks later...
Mommy: "I'm sorry, you were right, he tried to hurt your aunt."
Sixth Sense

Nightmare 101

How do I tell daddy?
Will he believe me?
Will he ask me, "why so long?"
What do I say to my sisters?
Did he touch them too?
Somebody please tell me it's all a nightmare,
pinch me and tell me it's not true.

What's wrong with you?

The alarm sounds: bathroom, makeup, hair, new
outfit, shoes and go.
Back home: closed blinds, crawl in bed, no food,
box of tissues and cry yourself to sleep.
On Repeat for three months
Knock, Knock,
Who is it?
Girl, what's wrong with you?

Mirror Reflection

What were you going to do?
You were eight!
I'm not eight anymore, no more nothing from
nobody!
Pushed and I'm pushing back harder.

Tears

I've cried so long and hard my face hurts.
Truth is that's the only thing I feel.
God am I turning cold or bold? I'm really not
sure.
If all I feel is warm tears running down my face,
please don't take the tears.

If I knew

If I knew I'd move mountains to save you.
If I'd known, I'd wrapped you in my arms and
never let go.
If I could buy back those years I would, but I
can't.
But I can tell you that your daddy is sorry.
If I knew...

I hate him!

God saved me at eight, you set out to destroy
me.
The potential was that fierce, that strong, that
intimidating?
You hate me? Or is it the force being birthed in
me?
Let's be clear, I hate you!

Transformation

I'm alive, I survived, I made it!
God, I'm done with asking why. Why me?
Help me see you, see your purpose in my pain.
Transform my mind, my heart. I am yours
fearfully and wonderfully made.

Forgiveness

A chain of bondage with so many links.
Links intertwined between me, my mind, and
them.
So many of them. So much deep rooted hurt,
pain and shame.
But I've got to be free.
I'll start with forgiving myself.

Statistics

I should be locked up, buried in somebody's
crazy house.
That's what the research says.
Bitter, battered, or beaten.
That's what my end was written to be.
I dropped statistics.

Favor

He was just a kid when I was hurt.
Always there on the playground, at the lunch
table.
My knight, my personal shield.
Always there in the shadows, yet visible when I
needed him.
My Christ-like Husband

Blessed

When life's choices and blows rip fruit from
your future, and leave you feeling flat, wait….
Because blessings come in their own incubating
time.

Gifts

You don't have to ask for my gift.
I give from my heart.
I'm not always understood, not because I'm
foreign, but because my love is.
Don't worry, there is nothing you could do to
change how I feel, even when you mistreat me,
my love will still be the same.

Learning to fly

It feels good having wind under my chin and not
a hand.
Are those clouds I see?

Powered

I don't need gas, oil, or electricity to move;
I've got 5 full faces with lashes, lips and big laughs.
Their love keeps me going.